HORSE FARM

AMERICAN QUARTER HORSES

ANNE ACCARDI

NorwoodHouse Press

Cataloging-in-Publication Data

Names: Accardi, Anne.
Title: American quarter horses / Anne Accardi.
Description: Buffalo, NY : Norwood House Press, 2027. | Series: Horse farm | Includes glossary and index.
Identifiers: ISBN 9781978580770 (pbk.) | ISBN 9781978580787 (library bound) | ISBN 9781978580794 (ebook)
Subjects: LCSH: Quarter horse--Juvenile literature.
Classification: LCC SF293.Q3 A33 2027 | DDC 636.133--dc23

Published in 2027 by
Norwood House Press
2544 Clinton Street
Buffalo, NY 14224

Designer: Rhea Magaro
Editor: Kim Thompson

Photo credits: Cover, p. 1 Lenkadan/Shutterstock.com; p. 5 Annabell Gsoedl/Shutterstock.com; p. 6 Library of Congress; p. 7 AnetaZabranska/Shutterstock.com; p. 8 Christy berry/Shutterstock.com; pp. 9-13 Jaco Wiid/Shutterstock.com; p. 14 Maros Bauer/Shutterstock.com; p. 15 D-VISIONS/Shutterstock.com; p. 17 Dagmara Ksandrova/Shutterstock.com; p. 18 Sabine Hagedorn/Shutterstock.com; p. 19 chaowalit jaiyen/Shutterstock.com; p. 21 Alla-V/Shutterstock.com;

Printed in the United States of America

CPSIA compliance information: Batch #CSNHP27: For further information contact Norwood House Press at 1-800-237-9932.

TABLE OF CONTENTS

Meet the American Quarter Horse 4
What Do Quarter Horses Look Like? 8
How Do Quarter Horses Help People? 12
What Do Quarter Horses Need? 18
Glossary 22
Thinking Questions 23
Index 24
About the Author 24

Meet the American Quarter Horse

The American quarter horse is a type of horse. It is the most popular horse **breed** in America.

5

These horses have been around for hundreds of years.

They got their name because they were bred to run quarter-mile races.

What Do Quarter Horses Look Like?

Their **coats** come in many colors.

Most are red, brown, black, or gray.

Like all horses, a quarter horse has a **mane**, a long tail, and four **hooves**.

These horses have short, wide heads. Their ears are small.

They have strong **muscles** for running.

How Do Quarter Horses Help People?

Quarter horses run very fast. People use them for racing.

They are best at **sprinting**. For short bursts, they can run as fast as a car on a highway.

Quarter horses are gentle and calm. This makes them good for riding.

Some people ride them in **rodeos**.

Some quarter horses work on **ranches**. They move supplies. People ride them to herd cows and sheep.

What Do Quarter Horses Need?

Quarter horses like to run. They need lots of open space!

They need healthy food. They eat grass, **hay**, and grains.

They should be **groomed** every day.
This keeps their coats clean and shiny.

Glossary

breed (breed): one type or kind of an animal

coats (kohts): the hair or fur that covers animals' bodies

groomed (groomd): combed, brushed, and cleaned

hay (hay): long grass that is cut, dried, and used as food for farm animals

hooves (hoovz): hard parts that cover the feet of horses, pigs, and other animals

mane (mayn): long, thick hair that grows on a horse's head and neck

muscles (MUHS-uhlz): body tissues that are attached to bones and that help people and animals move

ranches (RAN-chis): large farms where animals like cattle, sheep, and horses are raised

rodeos (ROH-dee-ohz): contests in which cowboys and cowgirls ride horses, rope calves, and do other tricks

sprinting (SPRIN-ting): running at top speed for a short distance

Thinking Questions

1. What colors can quarter horses be?
2. How did the American quarter horse get its name?
3. What are quarter horses used for?
4. How fast can quarter horses run?
5. Where could you find a quarter horse?

Index

colors 8

food 19

grooming 20

personality 14

races 7, 12

ranches 16

rodeos 15

running 7, 11, 12, 13, 18

About the Author

Anne Accardi is a librarian who loves reading books and learning new things! She lives in Kansas City, Missouri. When she's not writing, Anne enjoys listening to music, exploring nature around the city, and spending time with her family.